ELVIS

IS KING!

WRITTEN BY
JONAH WINTER

ILLUSTRATED BY
RED NOSE STUDIO

schwartz & wade books · new york

Elvis Is Born!

But alas, he is born
in a humble shack
on the wrong side of the railroad tracks,
the side where the poorest of the poor people live,
down down down in the Deep South—Tupelo, Mississippi.

Elvis's Daddy Is Arrested!

He forged a check—which is like stealing money.
Now he's got to go to jail,
leaving Elvis and his mama all alone
to fend for theyselves for fourteen months.
Times is hard.

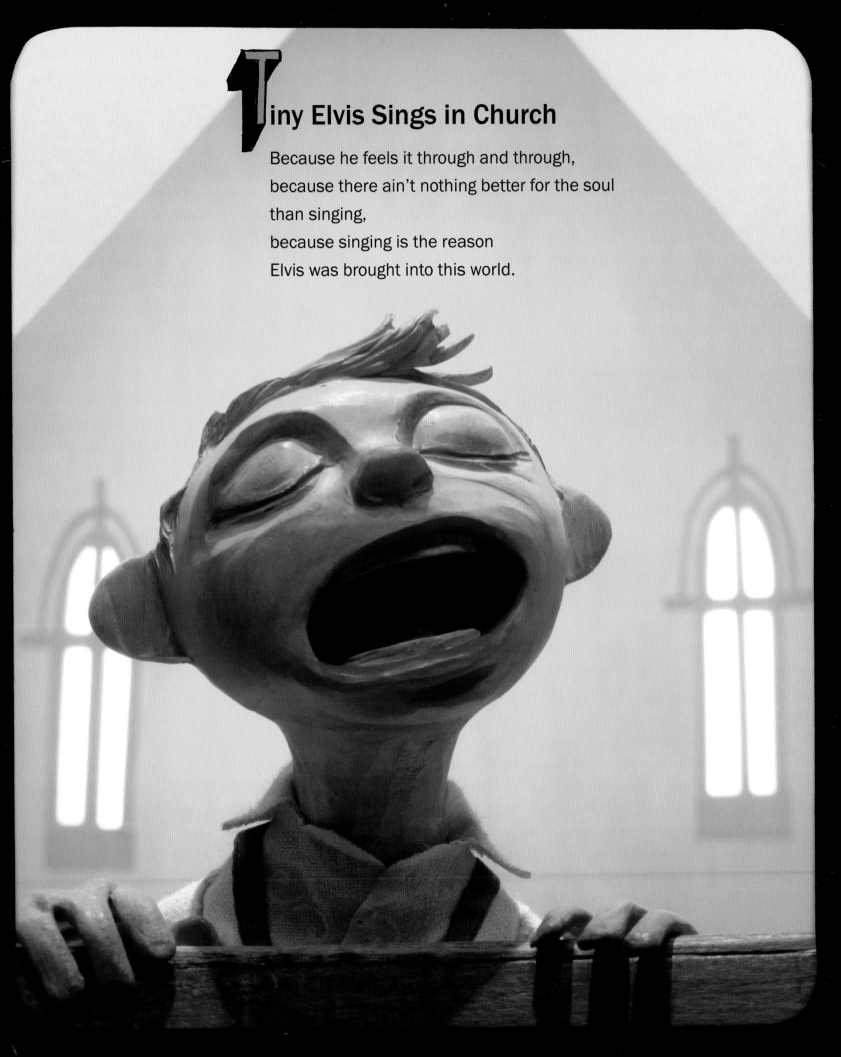

Tiny Elvis Sings in Church

Because he feels it through and through,
because there ain't nothing better for the soul
than singing,
because singing is the reason
Elvis was brought into this world.

County Fair Talent Show

Look at Little Elvis up onstage,

shy as he can be, ten years old,

so small he has to stand on a chair to reach the microphone,

but when he opens his mouth to sing—

a tearjerker song about a dog that dies—

everybody listens to every word. When he is done:

Clappin' and hootin'!

ELVIS IS LOVED!

What a feeling that is.

(Fifth Prize!)

Hardware Store Guitar

There it is, hanging from a strap
behind the counter.
With pennies she saved,
Mama buys her eleven-year-old birthday boy
the most important gift he will ever receive.
It will be the key to his salvation.

Elvis Sings in School

And he plays his little guitar, too.
All. The. Time.
Sure, it gets him in trouble.
But that's nothing
compared to the joy it brings him.

The Moment in the African American Church

From the dusty road,

Little Elvis hears some gospel singing,

goes to peek in the window,

and Good Lordy Mercy!

He ain't never heard nothin' that sweet before.

The First Cheeseburger Ever Eaten by Elvis

It is the first of many cheeseburgers Elvis will eat,

bought with pennies his mama has saved,

at the diner in tiny downtown Tupelo,

where everybody stares

'cause Mama ain't wearin' no shoes.

[snicker snicker snicker]

Exit from Tupelo

With all their belongings
packed into the rusty '39 Plymouth,
Mama, Papa, and thirteen-year-old Elvis
head for the open road to Memphis
to start a new life, hopefully a better one.
But on their first night there,
without enough money to buy even three cheeseburgers,
they dine on peanut butter and banana sandwiches—
in the car.
Which is also where they spend the night.

Elvis's First Apartment in Memphis

And so it goes:

Elvis, Mama, and Papa, all cooped up

in one dirty room,

sharing a bathroom down the hall with their neighbors.

It is in a rough part of town.

It is what they can afford.

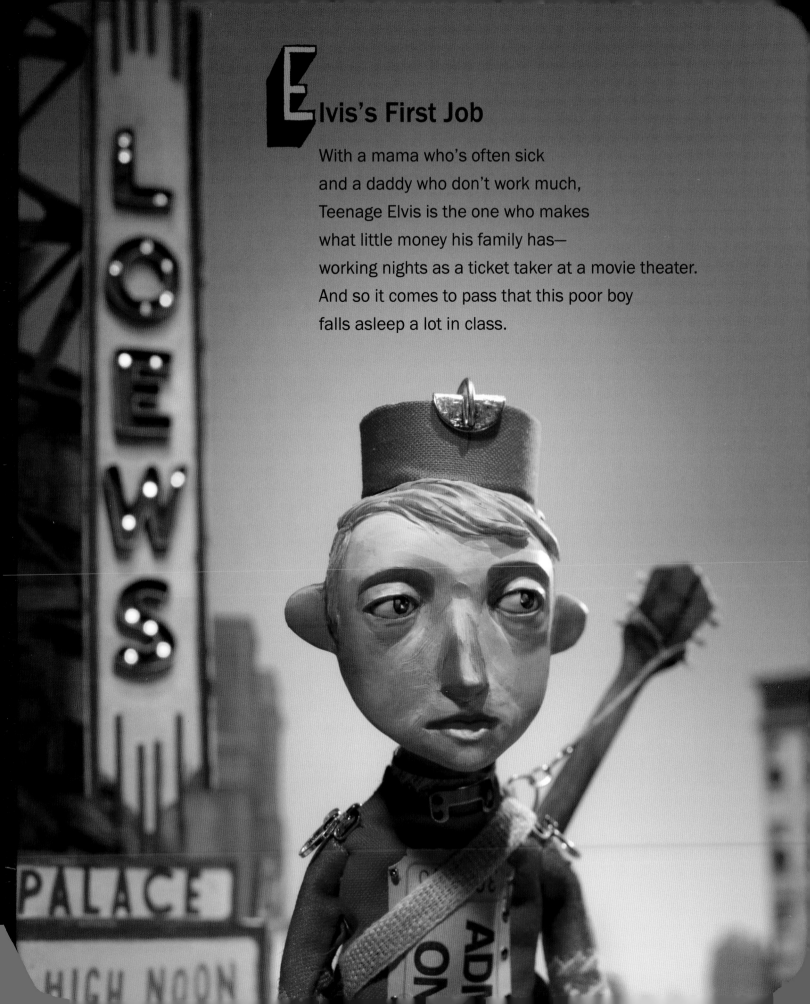

Elvis's First Job

With a mama who's often sick
and a daddy who don't work much,
Teenage Elvis is the one who makes
what little money his family has—
working nights as a ticket taker at a movie theater.
And so it comes to pass that this poor boy
falls asleep a lot in class.

"Train, Train, Comin' Round, Round the Bend . . ."

What would you do if you were just a poor country boy
in the big city, aching to be something more,
craving to be loved
the way a starving dog craves food?
What crazy plans might you concoct,
lying in bed at night,
listening to the freight trains passing by?

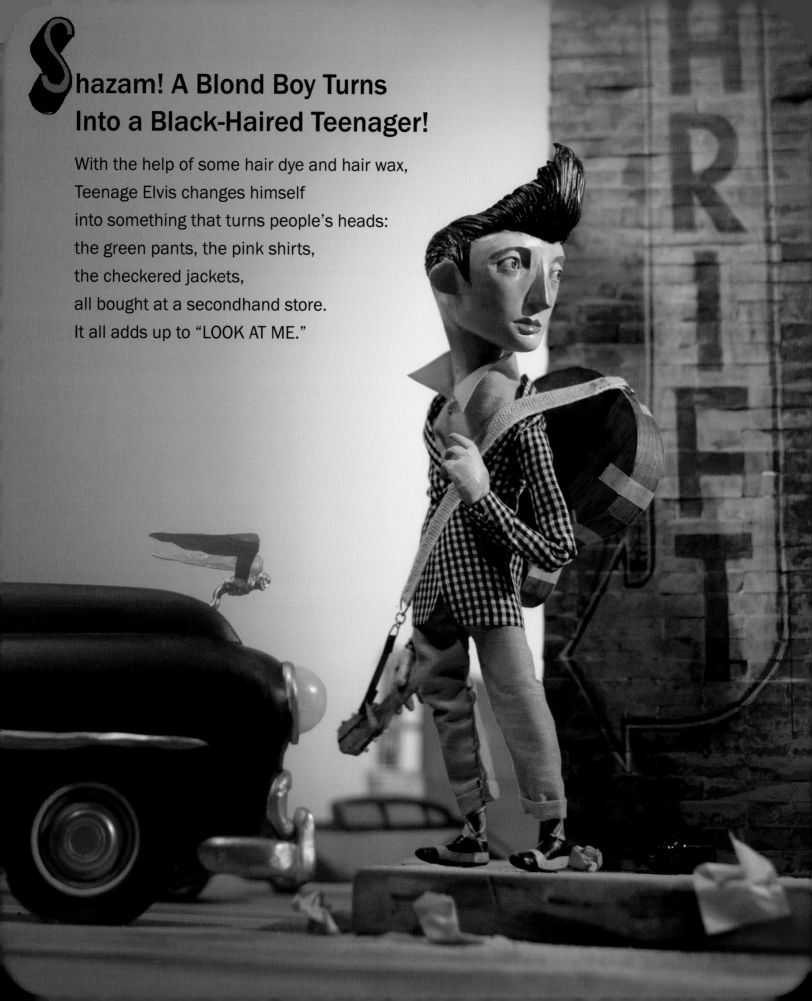

Shazam! A Blond Boy Turns Into a Black-Haired Teenager!

With the help of some hair dye and hair wax,
Teenage Elvis changes himself
into something that turns people's heads:
the green pants, the pink shirts,
the checkered jackets,
all bought at a secondhand store.
It all adds up to "LOOK AT ME."

High School Talent Show

Weird Teenage Elvis,
with his crazy hair and crazy clothes
and dirt-poor-country-boy shyness,
walks onstage with his guitar . . .
then KNOCKS 'EM DEAD with his song.
Something happens, something big, when he's up there:
He is no longer shy!
He can be whatever he wants to be—let loose, go crazy!
He feels loved!
And boy, does that feel good.

The First Love of Elvis

Her name is Dixie Locke
and just the sight of her
helps Tongue-Tied Teenage Elvis
relax and be himself andtalkandtalkandtalk
and wanna be with her forever and ever.

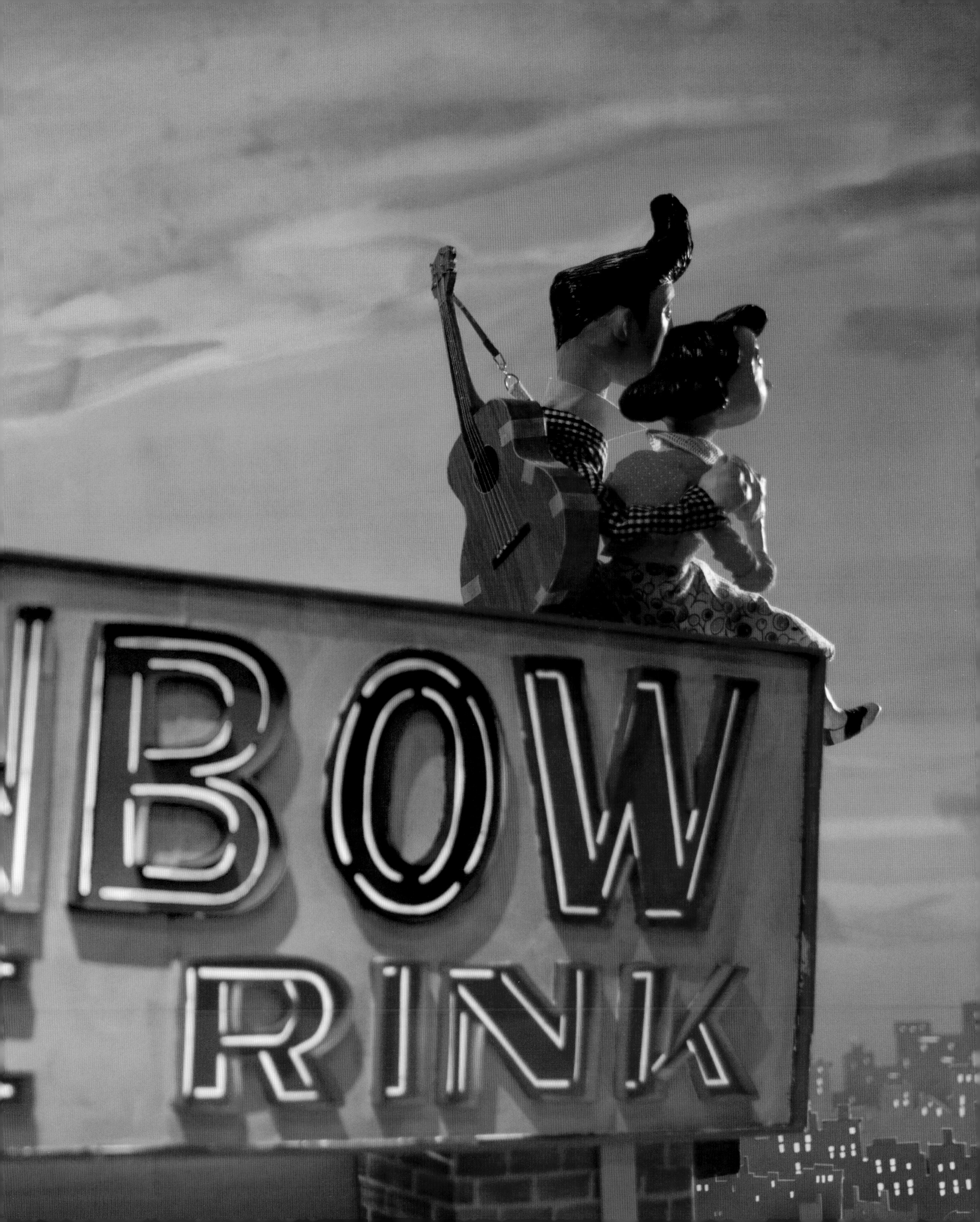
BOW
RINK

Beale Street Blues

Recent High School Graduate Elvis,
strolling in and strolling out
of every music club he passes,
listening to the blues, *feeling* the blues,
getting ideas for some blues he'd like to sing.

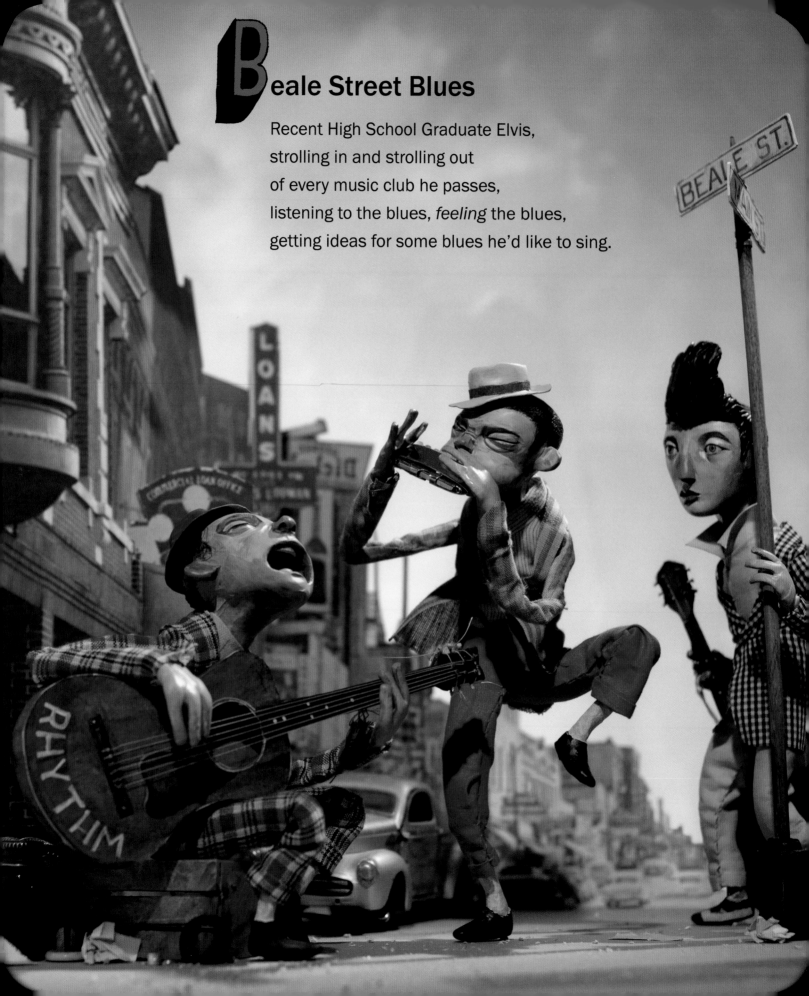

Elvis Publicly Declares His Mission in Life

Driving down the street,
he screeches to a halt,
jumps out of the car,
and yells,

"I'M GONNA BE THE BIGGEST STAR IN THE WORLD!"

The First Record

As a present for his mama,
Perfect Son Elvis goes downtown
to a place called Sun Studios,
where you can record yourself singing.
(It also makes *real* records of big-time singers—
and Sly Elvis knows this.)
The owner asks him who he sounds like.
"I don't sound like nobody," he says—
then pays her $3.98
to record a song called "My Happiness."
This is the First Song recorded by Elvis
(though no one hears it but a couple of people . . .).

MY HAPPINESS

Elvis Presley

"The Call" from the Record Company

When Tired Elvis gets home from his day job
driving a truck,
his mama tells him he got a call
(on the neighbor's phone—'cause they can't afford one).
It was from Sun Records—
they want Elvis to make a REAL RECORD!
That would be for sale!
Overjoyed Elvis jumps up and down
and walks on the ceiling and then flies!!!

Elvis Tries to Make a *Real* Record

But—he's just sitting in this chair,
not moving, not excited,
no feeling in his voice.
The recording guy just shakes his head.

Elvis Tries to Make a *Real* Record (Take Two)

So, Elvis and the other musicians are goofing around
during a break—having fun with a popular blues song
called "That's All Right."
Elvis is standing up now and shaking his hips
and doing these crazy moves with his knees
and making his voice all wobbly.
The recording guy perks up:
"LET'S RECORD *THAT*!"

First Elvis Song Ever Is Played on the Radio

But Elvis is nowhere to be seen.

He's hiding out in a movie theater.

He's scared.

What if people hate his song?

What if it's a flop?

First Elvis Song Ever Is Played on the Radio (Take Two)

Meanwhile, while Elvis is hiding in the dark,

teenagers are calling the radio station like crazy—

FIVE THOUSAND REQUESTS FOR "THAT'S ALL RIGHT"!!!

THE SONG IS PLAYED FIFTEEN TIMES IN ONE NIGHT!!!

PEOPLE ARE LOSING THEIR MINDS

OVER SOME PERSON NAMED ELVIS!!!

Something BIG is happening here.

The First Time the World Gets to See . . . the Brand-New Elvis

It's just a couple weeks later.

He's so nervous

he can't stop shaking,

even when he walks out onstage,

even when he starts to sing.

But that shaking, that shaking

starts an AVALANCHE of screaming—in a good way!

And so it begins: Brand-New Elvis now knows what to do onstage—

and he will never forget. It is a thing to behold.

The 147th Cheeseburger Eaten by Elvis

Boy, does that taste good—big and juicy,
ketchup and mustard oozing out of it.
And the best spice of all: success.
Girls come up to him, batting their starstruck eyes,
itching to get up close.
Mmmmmmmm-mmmm. . . .

1he First Heartbreak of Elvis

Good-Lookin' Heartthrob Elvis,
surrounded by girls, travelin' around,
is driftin' apart from his One True Love,
his little darlin', Dixie Locke.
And then it is over.
He will never love like that again.
Lovelorn Elvis is a heartbroken mess.
Now he's got something to sing about.
It is a blessing (in disguise).

"Heartbreak Hotel"

Unknown Outside of Memphis Elvis records a song about a sad hotel . . .

that rises to #1 on the pop charts.

NUMBER ONE!!!

All over America, people buy his record.

Elvis is rich!

Elvis is loved!

But the words to his song are:

"I'm so lonely, I get so lonely

I could die. . . ."

Arrival of the Screaming Teenage Girls

Somethin' 'bout the way he swivels his hips

and wiggles his knees

and curls his upper lip

and shakes his voice

and seems to be in love with each and every person in the audience

drives girls out of their MINDS.

They ain't never seen nothin' like this before.

No one has.

What Is This Crazy Music, Anyway?

Is it country music?

Sort of. But it's got too much of a BEAT.

Is it rhythm and blues?

Yep—a li'l bit!

It's blues, it's the music Elvis heard in the African American church—

it's black music sung by a Southern white man.

It's more than the sum of its parts.

It's rebellious and exciting

and something teenagers dig. It's . . .

ROCK 'N' ROLL, baby.

And Elvis is its KING—

THE BIGGEST STAR THE WORLD HAS EVER KNOWN!

# Author's Note

Elvis Presley was born on January 8, 1935, in Tupelo, Mississippi, to the impoverished Gladys and Vernon Presley, and he died at his mansion, Graceland, in Memphis, Tennessee, on August 16, 1977, one of the wealthiest and most famous performing musicians in history. It would be hard to name a more classic rags-to-riches story than that of Elvis, who is still known as the King of Rock 'n' Roll.

What is most amazing is just how fast Elvis went from being a shy, stuttering teenager to being on top of the pop music world. It was on July 5, 1954, at the age of nineteen, that he recorded his first real record, "That's All Right." Just a year and a half later, in January 1956, he recorded his first #1 hit, "Heartbreak Hotel." In September of that year, he made his first television appearance on the very popular *Ed Sullivan Show.* No one had ever seen anything like Elvis on TV before. His swiveling hips and crazy moves caused such a stir with (female) members of the studio audience that during a future appearance, the cameras focused on him only from the waist up. And in November, *Love Me Tender,* the first of thirty-one movies in which he would star, was released. By this point, it was official: Elvis was the biggest music star in America—and he was still only twenty-one years old!

It is undeniable that Elvis owed much of his success to the essential fact that he was white during an era of massive discrimination against African Americans, an era when the music world was blatantly segregated. The first person to record him, Sam Phillips of Sun Records, absolutely was looking for a white musician to play "black music" for white teenagers. In that first recording session, just messing around with "That's All Right" (written and recorded by African American rhythm and blues musician Arthur Crudup in 1946), Elvis gave Phillips exactly what he was looking for. And he continued to give Phillips white versions of black songs—with another early hit, "Mystery Train" (quoted in this story: "Train, Train, Comin' Round, Round the Bend"), written by black blues star Junior Parker for Sun Records.

Elvis took inspiration from anywhere he could find it—rhythm and blues, gospel, country and western, and crooners. The B side of the vinyl record that contained "That's All Right" was a cover of the bluegrass song "Blue Moon of Kentucky," which Elvis transformed into a fast-paced rockin' number. Elvis's rockin' approach did not go over well at the Grand Ole Opry, which is sort of like the national "cathedral" of country music.

But even if Elvis's music offended country music purists, he was always at heart a country boy. And this is why I have included Southern dialect here and there. I am from the South, and my ancestors are from Mississippi and Alabama. My Texas grandmother, one of my favorite people of all time, used to say "Good Lordy Mercy!"—as do many people from this part of the world. I included such phrases out of love and compassion.

As a teenager in the 1970s, I was way more into 1950s rock 'n' roll than the music of the time. I especially loved Chuck Berry and Little Richard, who had as much if not more to do with inventing rock as Elvis. But oh, did I love Elvis! His voice made me feel something deep inside my gut. It made me want to sing along (something I only did, thankfully, behind my bedroom door). And I will confess to still channeling my inner Elvis occasionally, belting out one of his early songs when no one's around.

Why do so many people, including me, still get turned on by Elvis's music? Because his early songs, especially, are outrageously exciting and full of energy: songs like "Hound Dog," "Jailhouse Rock," "Don't Be Cruel," and "All Shook Up." And his music is full of real feeling; it's personal. There are photos of Elvis in his early twenties that show him to be miserable, overwhelmed, just a country boy who's suddenly found himself on top of the world—a scary place to be. Though he was always surrounded by friends and fans, Elvis remained a lonely man throughout his life, unable to get close to anyone. And yet this lonely man was one of the most charismatic performers of all time. When he was onstage, something he was doing with his voice and his body, revealing emotions that were so raw, released emotions in his audience. It was like he had turned on a spigot, and the tears and the screams and the unnamed feelings just came pouring out. His music gave his original audience—mainly 1950s white teenagers—the freedom to *feel*.

Why is Elvis still called the King? Listen to his music, watch film clips of his performances, especially from the 1950s, and see for yourself.

Elvis Presley with his parents, 1937
Michael Ochs Archives / Stringer

Scene from the movie *Jailhouse Rock,* 1957
Rue Des Archives / Bridgeman Images

Presley Signing Autographs, 1956
Bettmann / Contributor

For a look-inside video, and more, visit ElvisIsKingExtras.com.

For Luca —J.W.

For the stars who have yet to shine —R.N.S.

Text copyright © 2019 by Jonah Winter

Jacket art and interior illustrations copyright © 2019 by Red Nose Studio

All rights reserved. Published in the United States by Schwartz & Wade Books, an imprint of Random House Children's Books, a division of Penguin Random House LLC, New York.

Schwartz & Wade Books and the colophon are trademarks of Penguin Random House LLC.

Visit us on the Web! rhcbooks.com

Educators and librarians, for a variety of teaching tools, visit us at RHTeachersLibrarians.com

Library of Congress Cataloging-in-Publication Data

Name: Winter, Jonah, author. | Red Nose Studio, illustrator.

Title: Elvis is King! / by Jonah Winter ; illustrated by Red Nose Studio.

Description: First edition. | New York : Schwartz & Wade Books, [2019]

Identifiers: LCCN 2018008797 (print) | LCCN 2018009654 (ebook) | ISBN 978-0-399-55472-8 (Ebook)

ISBN 978-0-399-55470-4 (hardcover) | ISBN 978-0-399-55471-1 (library binding)

Subjects: LCSH: Presley, Elvis, 1935–1977—Juvenile literature.

Rock musicians—United States—Biography—Juvenile literature.

Classification: LCC ML3930.P73 (ebook) | LCC ML3930.P73 W56 2019 (print)

DDC 782.42166092 [B]—dc23

The text of this book is set in Franklin Gothic Book.

The illustrations are hand-built three-dimensional sets shot with a

Canon EOS 5D MarkIII Digital SLR camera. The initial capital letters were drawn with

a Hunt 108 pen nib, small brushes, and Higgins Black Magic ink on paper.

MANUFACTURED IN CHINA

2 4 6 8 10 9 7 5 3 1

First Edition